Breath and Shadow

Six-Sentence Stories

Breath and Shadow

Six-Sentence Stories

Robert Scotellaro
& Meg Pokrass

MadHat Press
Cheshire, Massachusetts

MadHat Press
MadHat Incorporated
PO Box 422, Cheshire, MA 01225

The Library of Congress has assigned
this edition a Control Number of
2024940099

ISBN 978-1-952335-84-6 (paperback)

Words by Robert Scotellaro & Meg Pokrass
Cover image: *Lake George Reflection* by Georgia O'Keeffe, c. 1921
Cover design by Marc Vincenz

www.MadHat-Press.com

First Printing
Printed in the United States of America

Table of Contents

Robert Scotellaro
Section One

Misfits 3
Atlas Wasn't Giving Anything Away 4
Spectacles 5
This Heat! 6
Put a Lid on It 7
The Proud Parents of Light 8
Tattoo 9
Topiary 10
Two-Way Mirror 11
After 12

Meg Pokrass
Section Two

Cat Proposal 15
Man Made of Hours 16
Dwarves at the Door 17
Decanter Gig 18
Dad Shadows 19
In the Flower Library 20
Old Selves 21
The Forest 22
Dangerous Excavation 23
Whoopee, Hallelujah! 24

Robert Scotellaro
Section Three

Air Cello 27
A Treachery of Metaphors 28
Dollhouse Furniture 29
To an Old Pair of Shoes 30

Horney 31
The Cult Leader's Clockworks 32
5,000-Inch TV and the Rain 33
Dainty 34
The Whatchamacallit 35
Vegetable Porn 36

Meg Pokrass
Section Four

Gifts 39
Acting-School Lessons 40
Bob's Belly 41
Heron Sighting 42
Don't Bother, They're Here 43
Hips 44
Pond Life 45
Moon Realization 46
Colorful 47
Classic Movie Husband Arrival 48

Robert Scotellaro
Section Five

Terror Tatts 51
Medusas from Outer Space 52
The Limits of Frost 53
Who We Are and Who We Wish to Be 54
How Porn Stars Pick Their Names 55
Counterbalance 56
Kamasutra for Virgins 57
Squeezebox Serenade 58
Swimming Hole 59
Coming Clean 60

Meg Pokrass
Section Six

Luck 63
Pictures of Extreme Discomfort 64
Girls 65
Let's Not Use the Word "Delicious" 66
Clouds before and after you were born 67
Bones 68
Gone 69
As We Fade 70
The Wig Talks 71
Extraterrestrial 72

Robert Scotellaro
Section Seven

Count On It 75
The Dentist and the Peanut Lady 76
Accompaniment 77
Interpreter of Dreams 78
High Up/Low Down 79
A Penchant for Renegades 80
Newfound 81
A Visit from Bad News 82
Excerpts from a Gangbanger's Diary 83
Subterranean 84

Meg Pokrass
Section Eight

Coral Reef Hotel 87
Blood Lines 88
Diet Commercial 89
Auld Lang Syne Syndrome 90
The Nice Christmas 91
Embracing the Waves 92
Twigs 93

Empty Driveway 94
Sex and Wild Seed 95
Extraction Dream 96

Robert Scotellaro
Section Nine

My Father Takes Up Juggling 99
Paper Roses for the Fire God 100
Adjustments 101
Post Facto 102
Crosscurrents 103
Upper and Lower Universes 104
My Mother's Parting Words to My Father 105
The Ghost Whisperer 106
Why Some Men Talk and Spit 107
Knotty Pine 108

Meg Pokrass
Section Ten

The dog sniffed you out 111
Moonlighting 112
Cotton-Candy Truth 113
Moon Blindness 114
Paper-Doll Men 115
Fun Done 116
Wrong Birds 117
Knee-Deep 118
Endorphins 119
Fillmore Street 120

Acknowledgments 121
About the Authors 123

A human being is only breath and shadow.

—Sophocles

Robert Scotellaro

Section One

Misfits

She didn't wear makeup, said it was for clowns and dead people. We were smoking cigarettes with our backs against the high red diner seats, back when they'd let you. She was the freaky kid in school, and I was her only friend, and she was the only one who'd listen to my poetry. Her kisses were wild, but she spoke softly, told me she believed in alien abductions, that they took her uncle, but everyone knew her uncle crossed the wrong people in a drug deal and was under a bunch of leaves somewhere in the woods. She listened to my poetry and I listened to her thoughts on extraterrestrial thievery, and that worked for us. We laughed a lot, and I didn't mind the tattoo spider crawling out of her blouse, or the dirty looks the waitress was giving us, clutching her pad and holding up her pencil like it was the friggin' torch and she was the Statue of Liberty—like she was all that.

Atlas Wasn't Giving Anything Away

I told my father I played a duet with God once, and it was spectacular. That I played a mean harmonica, and God played a conga beat on an upside-down trashcan. Well, it wasn't really my father, just a framed photo of him with me as a kid on his shoulders. I never mentioned the LSD, but figured if his ghost ever showed I'd square it with him. "You know, I always wanted to skydive while playing an accordion," I said, gazing at the beefy breadth of him, that top-of-the-world view I had from there. I wondered what it was he wanted to do but never did, before he slid the world from his shoulders, clicked on the TV and hid inside all that canned laughter.

Spectacles

There they were, his reading glasses at the bottom of the clear toilet-bowl water, neatly folded. There was something sad and tragic about the sight of them, something bigger drowned. She had been hounding him again the night before about having a baby as he was reading in bed, and he just waved her off, turning the page and saying it wasn't the right time. He could hear some clock (some Big Ben) gonging in her, rattling the headboard and making the lampshade tilt. He put his hand down into the shallow water and retrieved them, brought them to the sink to rinse. Put them on streaked and dripping and allowed himself to see the world that way.

This Heat!

I was near the rim of the volcano with my lashes singed and never felt more alive. Samantha was many feet behind, cursing me, saying, "This heat, this heat!" Later, under a wobbly ceiling fan, we made love, and there was a little something extra in it. Outside we sat on fruit crates and tried to breathe the bigger block of air and drank tequila straight from the bottle. A dog with three legs sidled past and then dropped down in a wedge of sunlight and slept. Samantha kept saying how her face still burned, but I was busy watching the creature twitching through some dreamscape, strangely envying it.

Put a Lid on It

He felt sometimes as though he was made of paper and there was no room between the raindrops. He told her that, and she grabbed a handful, told him, "That doesn't feel anything like paper to me." They'd met at a bar in town and were in his vintage Bullet camper by a small seasonal stream. He thought to himself: *What the fuck, did that actually come out of my mouth?* He puffed out his chest and the Spanish war ship on it expanded a bit. He hoped she wouldn't notice the stack of poetry books by the side of his bed.

The Proud Parents of Light

When I was young my mother took me to visit The Proud Parents of Light. There were candles everywhere. "Look how beautiful the shadows are," my mother said. A breeze came in an open window and The Proud Parents of Light tapped their feet as if to music as the candles wavered and the shadows danced. The candles were bright, the shadows stark, and they were inextricably bound. Decades later I'd wonder if there was some metaphor/lesson my mother wished to impart, but she was The Proud Parent of My Ignorance, she told me and felt there was no reason, whatsoever, to rush things.

Tattoo

He got the tattoo overseas where there was a war, in a country where he wasn't welcomed. He could barely walk straight, walk at all, the gin doing something funny with his legs when he got it. The tattoo was in black Asian characters he'd thought represented something noble, as he requested: "Free Spirit" but it translated more accurately as: "refrigerator mold." Years later he told his impatient daughter it meant *Good things come to those who wait.* He told his reckless son it meant *Look before you leap.* He told his wife it meant *Forever faithful*—depending completely on them never comparing notes.

Topiary

Peggy's phone rings and she jumps; she is a 911 emergency operator and this is her day off, but there is a tether she cannot cut. It's her mother complaining again about the people upstairs—"They must be bowling up there," her mother says—"dear god!" Peg hardly listens: there is no one bleeding out, crushed under a car, unable to get those last few breaths ... Since Brad passed she's been cuddling up to the bottle—any bottle—the label doesn't matter. She goes out on the deck after with her latest fluid companion and watches Mike next door look over the hedge at her with his clippers open and that married man's flirty grin. Topiary art, he calls it pointing out an indistinguishable castle tower, the humped backs of two elephants, but she sees a phallus, and two large breasts, unaccountably false promises, a cheap motel, an outstretched hand, and coy-widow smiles back at him.

Two-Way Mirror

His shoes squeaked when he walked. He had no idea why or how to keep them from doing so. She said she liked a good pair of shoes with something to say, this new woman in his life. He wore mirrored sunglasses to be cool, and she looked into them to fix her hair, never seeing what saw her. Her shoes were quiet like most shoes, and she told him how great that was, how opposites attract. During sex she had him wear the mirrored sunglasses, and though she missed the squeaking shoes quiet by the bed, she quite enjoyed the way those two adoring eyes gazed back at her.

After

Songbirds fly through my window screen and come out the other end, grated. Lightbulbs melt like wickless candles, making darkness their unwitting companions. My shoes turn into steam irons as I hop about the room spot-pressing the carpet. I hear the gods pissing on my roof and want to believe it is rain. Lava runs down a mountain out back that wasn't there a moment earlier, with its chili-pepper mouths eating up the landscape. I never should have taken that call.

Meg Pokrass

Section Two

Cat Proposal

This is the night you propose to the cat. She has nothing left to prove to you—is wild and pale and her eyes are green as pickles. You know there are parts of your heart that you can offer her fluffy light spirit. You have stopped answering the phone, made changes to your will. *Snowball,* you say. Just the sound of her name is a wedding gown.

Man Made of Hours

In the Museum of Time you stand there staring at a grandfather clock. It has a smooth face, like a man you used to believe in. There are fathers and husbands everywhere you look, living in the faces of these clocks. The curator walks over, looks at you as if you might have suffered a stroke. *What makes you think you've been dreaming these guys up?* she asks, taking your hand in hers with the papery feel of dried leaf. The two of you and your wrinkly hands, staring at the museum of everything you have ever wanted.

Dwarves at the Door

Seven hungry-looking dwarves knock on your door, so you invite them in for cookies. The first thing you notice is how each of them has a sad story to tell. All of their stories have to do with their fathers, who have died. All of them miss their fathers grievously, and weep while telling you about it. They try not to look at each other because they are men. They regret that they never told their fathers how much they loved them, so they tell it to you instead.

Decanter Gig

Her job was being paid to follow an elderly widow around her own house. The client had a depressed waxy smile, one that seemed stuck on her face since she lost her husband in the flood. There were the heavy sighs from the toilet, and they floated around her ears. She would stand there, just outside the door while the woman allowed all of her sadness to dribble out. The sound was like something you'd find in nature. "Shhh," the old woman would say, "I'm letting go of him again."

Dad Shadows

How could we not find one potential dad on the highway? We drove slowly, taking turns at the wheel, stopping only when hunger like a mother asked us to sit down and eat. And sometimes there were large masculine shadows following us into convenience stores to buy HoHos or Tandytakes or Butterscotch Twinkles, the sustenance of life! We were getting bigger in order to feel small again. Any one of them could do it, we thought. It would be so easy.

In the Flower Library

In the flower library, she remains a tendril. Taking her father away from her mother again and again, transplanting him. Her father saying, *Don't encourage your mother's madness,* talking to her like she's already in bloom. In the library, she is a rare orchid, the kind that blooms where it shouldn't. The kind of flower that men take care of, but only for a while. How beautiful this flower library is, she thinks, so full of specimens that never quite opened up all the way.

Old Selves

There you were humming them songs. There you were feeling fat inside your clothes even though you were tiny. There you were in the midst of your one-time-only beauty, a beauty you'd rent for a decade and then decide it had been enough.

There you were in your mother's house, the one she loved because it was her own and she could tear down walls and build cupboards, the one she'd have to sell when she got cancer.

There you were at the end of childhood, still loving your mother too much and trying not to let it ruin you.

There you were baking cookies for the relatives, listening to "Lovely Rita," thinking about how great it will feel to be a sexy meter maid.

The Forest

It has something to do with the adoption of that unwanted animal, right there in the living room. Her husband watching telly, drinking beer, not looking at the animal dancing around. The animal gazing into her eyes, finding her interesting and rare. Later, she makes a list of things she cannot do to please him. Increasingly she falls asleep in the forest next to the animal. His sharp nose against her throat, his wet, dark breath becoming her own.

Dangerous Excavation

A middle-aged psychiatrist wants to unearth the actual woman from a deep hole in which she lives. "How lovely and strange you are," he tries not to say to her, while she is lounging on the sofa in his office. He stares out the window, hoping for one bright red bird. Wonders aloud, "Who, then, is the real patient? And why the hell does she wear such terrible glasses?" He wonders these things, in his securely married way.

Whoopee, Hallelujah!

After a month with the psychic, Dad slunk home. Said he'd been in a trance but the spell finally broke. "I'm home in exactly one piece."

Mom glared, said "Whoopee Hallelujah!"

Took Dad's hand and the two of them hip-bumped down toward the tracks. Only then did I hear the train.

ROBERT SCOTELLARO

SECTION THREE

Air Cello

There's a woman on the bus playing air cello. Who does such a thing? Her flexible face translates the profundity of such an instrument/a moment, as she bows and presses strings beyond invisibility. The melody is nearly familiar and one needs wine or whiskey to wash it down. Her eyes are closed, yet she sees/we see, each other. A young man with his baseball cap on backward boards and plays a screechy air guitar with his face twisted, and the spell is broken—but it's all right; it's my stop anyway.

A Treachery of Metaphors

Metaphors in disguise come to my door to rough me up, or at least threaten to. They are all from poems I have written about my father and he has paid them well. I rip the fake moustache off one, a wig from another, as they look away sheepishly. "And I thought I could trust you, all of you," I say as they slink off. Later, at my desk, a simile taps at my window with its beak and flares out a wide expanse of rudderless wings. It has something red at the end of its beak, has sincere watery eyes, and, cautiously, I let it in.

Dollhouse Furniture

He was a tugboat captain. And built like one. Short and barrel-chested with the buttons of his shirt perpetually stressed. He said he moved ocean liners about as easily as dollhouse furniture, and hoped he didn't come off as overcompensating. "Can you move me?" she said, and leaned in. There was something about that smile, the full stretch of those glossy red lips, the way she held her drink even, at an angle without spilling a drop, that made him wonder.

To an Old Pair of Shoes

I told my old pair of shoes that I was sorry, but it was time. Time for the trash and that I knew they deserved better. Maybe nothing military where rifles were fired into the air and a flag was folded into a triangle, but that they'd been through the wars. Walked into doorways and out of them, dragged me along through sorrow and joy. Paced the rug and danced upon it, roamed streets through rosy neon/through sunlight in their sheen. Lay beside a lover's bed, always patient, always waiting for a new direction, their last now, into that cold indiscriminate barrel amongst inglorious leavings, with nowhere else left to go.

Horney

When his wife wore the moose antlers to bed he knew she'd found out about Lilly. He wasn't going to risk an eye, so he kept his distance; *mea culpas* didn't help. After a time, she downsized to goat horns and he stretched a tentative arm out. Then came the foam rubber devil horns, soft as cotton and he really started to worry. It was that asshole from Accounts Pending he'd seen her lock eyeballs with as if they were Crazy Glued. But he figured fair is fair and slid the rhinoceros horn cap he had by his side of the bed, under it, swallowed that bitter pill and made his way over, with safe passage, to all that warmth.

The Cult Leader's Clockworks

"It's harder than you think. And I keep running out of ways to explain things. Long for that chicken farm in the middle of nowhere, the isolation, all those eggs hatching or bubbling in the pan. But they love/need me and I love that sharky vintage Cadillac with the pointy fins and the dark windows like a magic trick that makes you disappear. And who could ever deny them that *hunger*: the way they swing like playground kids on every word."

5,000-Inch TV and the Rain

Testosterone was a thing in the room you could store in big barrels. The men were watching the game on that new 5,000-inch TV Ray had to have. Two other men splintered off and were arm-wrestling on a small card table that kept tipping, as the one with big biceps and a panther tattoo clawing up one of them kept eyeballing Rita. Ray repeatedly asked her for more beer and she told him she didn't see any crutches, which made his friends laugh at him as he glared at her. She went outside in the rain, stood there feeling washed somewhat and knew she would leave him, but the *how* and *when* eluded her. She tried to light a cigarette, needed to light a cigarette, but couldn't—each drop was whale-sized and it was pouring.

Dainty

Her mother called the place she was in "a palace for peculiars." Her daughter called it a nuthouse, but never out loud. On good days, visiting, the daughter called it "temporary," on bad, *necessary*. There were roses (lawn chairs among them to sit in)—their reliable beauty. The mother still had her hankies while everyone else used tissues. They were dainty, embroidered at the edges, monogramed, and the daughter remembered how her mother would put a finger at their center and gently dab a tear away from her little-girl eyes—the pain of the world away—one at a time, how simple an act/a remedy that was.

The Whatchamacallit

He made balloon animals for the tourists at Pier 39 in San Francisco: dachshunds, rabbits, and occasionally an amorphous and elaborate "thing" he called a *whatchamacallit,* which was open to interpretation, and his one squeaky plunge at being an artist. He dated my sister at the time and told me once he felt like the head of an unstruck match with all that fire inside. I asked him one day what his "whatchamacallit" was and he just laughed and blew up a few long skinny balloons, and with a robust twisting fury, created something extraordinary. Something, that if it had not been made of that taut, ephemeral skin, was made of something durable and lasting, might be showcased in a gallery or museum. He smiled and put the *thing* on the coffee table, then clicked on the TV to watch the game, but all I could watch was that complex and extraordinary construction with the ineffable sum of its twists and turns. And his breath trapped inside it.

Vegetable Porn

She picks up a large zucchini, seems to fondle it, appraises its size and shape, slides a hand up and down the length of it. He's certain she knows he is watching. He is by a low pyramid of beefsteak tomatoes and picks one up and squeezes it gently, turns a bit toward her. He goes back and takes another, one in each hand, rotating them slowly. The woman doesn't notice the man, the tomatoes, but only the little fingernail half-moons in the green skin of the zucchini and thinks, how utterly *uncivilized* that anyone should have handled it so recklessly, so wantonly.

Meg Pokrass

Section Four

Gifts

Why wouldn't he want to make love to her, for God's sake? She could yodel, perform bird calls on cue, the way real birds understood them. Could fold a stained dish towel into a hat, was gypsy-pretty, had a dog-friendly hatchback car that didn't smell. Was great at making people laugh about her ex-husband's phobias. Would say, "I loved him so much that I had to divorce him." So many gifts.

Acting-School Lessons

As part of the Stanislavsky acting method, and to get into our roles, we nuns walked casually over to a local cemetery where dead people lived. It was as close to a nunnery as we could get. All 12 of us walked around silently. We smoked and we tried not to get depressed. We sat near the tombstones and bonded with dead people. I sat near the stone of a woman named Angela Mary Jones, who died at age 43. I imagined myself at age 43, alive yet dead, married to someone who loved me for having failed at the roles I loved most.

Bob's Belly

After his ex gave up and took off, it felt like a festering splinter had been removed. Just terrible, how a woman could undermine a man's confidence like that, Bob thought. He knew that from here on in, solitude was going to be the only sane solution. "Mary had perfection issues," he told his belly, who growled in harmonious agreement. Bob and his belly were once again a team. He enjoyed setting it free on a warm summer's day, watching it wobble in the sun.

Heron Sighting

At the airport you met up with his Great Blue Heron. It has been slouching near a nasty spill of chili-fries in the first-floor café. This was the café where he'd left you (and the bird) with a two-hour wait before boarding the plane. His ex was at the hospital and his phone kept ringing. He buzzed and limped through the airport as though hobbled by sound. "She'll never stop trying to win him back, will she?" you said to that disoriented bird.

Don't Bother, They're Here

"Hon, they're here!" you said, referring to the clowns, who were pounding on our door.

You were tearing around trying to straighten the place up while I stood there completely still. We were tired, smiling with relief.

"There should always be clowns," you said, pouring out the gin.

I had recently been thinking, *aren't we a pair?* and here they were, just like before.

"Get your sorry old selves back in here and look at this mess," I said, ushering them in, telling them to sit on the stained sofa, not to bother removing their coats.

Hips

My hips? The hips of a small, uncomfortable bird. Hers? Invisible, and when we rode our bikes, those bones took us out of the craziest places, away from our stepfather who stared, from our mother who never trusted her own winged breadth. We could fly on our bikes, think about how little it mattered. We learned to survive on water and melba toast, so skinny we wobbled like palm trees.

Pond Life

Hello, old friend, hello, she said. She swallowed it back, then looked around to see if anyone noticed how long she stood there by the pond. Gulping and staring. She had hunted for this fish all her life. Yes to the flap of tail, yes to his unflattering pink gills. Yes to curling and probing the pond of its actual life.

Moon Realization

"Keep a lookout for Nessie," he said, "where it's deepest in the middle of the loch; don't let your eyes wander." His front tooth was chipped, and only in the moonlight did she recognise that something had hurt him. "What kind of creature did that to you?" she asked, but her words got lost in the night.

"Who, who?" he hooted, so she pretended not to hear him, pretended that his words were nothing but the call of an uncatchable owl. Late in the night, they clutched each other. The warmth of his shoulder made her skin feel like feathers.

Colorful

In the end: she was too colorful. He couldn't abide it. Shocking blue eyelids, purple lips, gold swirls beneath brows. She thought she could add hues to his life, wake him up with her orange-monkey smile. "Is there one specific shade that worries you?" she'd say while he stood there in his mouse-brown sweatshirt, staring as if she were about to strike. Even the roof of her house, rain-drenched, flashed stolen treasure.

Classic Movie Husband Arrival

I ordered the Rhett Butler on a Black Friday because my Ashley Wilkes broke as soon as I unwrapped him. The Rhett arrived on Saturday morning, frowning at my lackluster life. "Miss O'Hara, your drain needs snaking. A bourbon when nothing else will do." He popped a grin, chugged, and poured me one—so I sat there next to him, warming my bones. "They say you've been manless here since Atlanta burned, little honey, and don't expect me, cheap even with overnight delivery, to fix it."

Robert Scotellaro

Section Five

Terror Tatts

She was a one-nighter, had gruesome tattoos crouched under her clothes. It was a quick and somewhat disconcerting excavation: all those blood-dripping teeth and claws of real and imagined angry beasts. But she liked a lot of the same poets I did, could even quote stanzas, and what dwelled inside did not reflect what terrorized her skin. She told me she was struck twice by lightning, which somehow freed her, was a barmaid at the end of the world. I looked to see if her face would change, but it didn't. I never pursued either claim, just cuddled up beside a gaping maw, some inky pack of daunting creatures, just to feel the warmth beneath them.

Medusas from Outer Space

He's writing a novel where Medusas from outer space, with snakes hissing from their heads, take over the world. "Dystopia is always in fashion," he tells his ex-wife, as he's there to pick up their daughter for the weekend, and she gazes at him with that jaw-to-the-floor long look that was too often present when they were together. He's brought three new Barbies for their child, holds them like a bouquet. As he describes the crazed Medusas' snakes biting only the powerful men of the world, she wonders if there isn't some other kind of venom involved. "That's good," she says, "I can imagine the movie," knowing she has already seen it the other way around.

The Limits of Frost

My sister, rebel-hardened as a teen, skated on my father's icy looks. Those bandoliers crisscrossing the front of her as the blades of her ice skates glided along his cold stares. His sternness trying to chill-force her short skirts into lengthening. Her hard rock music into softening. Even that walk-in freezer he had for a head, she'd enter, find the frozen beer spills on the floor and twirl on them with the door open for her audience: me and my mom to see—the lovely blur she'd become. Doing a flawless triple Lutz, a double axel despite my father's querulous groans, gliding across that stone-hard ice that never melted.

Who We Are and Who We Wish to Be

The Woman of My Dreams is walking down the street holding a canary in a cage. She stops by a store that is having a bed and mattress sale and looks in the window. I gaze in too, follow her eyes to the bed I'd pick/we'd pick for our lives together. She and her canary look at me and the bird sings the loveliest tune. My parrot in the cage I'm holding sings (a euphemism) a crusty sea chanty with lots of foul language and breast-out bird bravado, and I smile sheepishly. The Woman of My Dreams walks away with her portable jukebox, and I tell myself I've got to stop hanging out at that wharf bar, continue looking through the pane at that bed, consider how empty it looks without us.

How Porn Stars Pick Their Names

She picked the biggest asshole in the bar she could find, determined this would be revenge sex in payment for all those years of *knowing*. The kids were grown, but she still had her figure and the dim lighting subtracted what the years had added. She had a voice that was soft and soothing, made stress reduction tapes professionally, and the man across from her kept saying he couldn't hear her above the music. Three drinks in he told her how porn stars got their names: "you pick the name of your first pet and the street name of the first place you ever lived," determined hers would be: Fluffy Chattanooga, and he laughed. She peered at him and spoke, sotto voce, with that calming cadence: "you fucking twit, you brainless hulk, you piece of shit: you're nothing but a cock and my venom." He leaned in, nearly knocking over his drink: "What?" he said—what?—it's pretty loud in here; you'll have to speak up, darlin.'"

Counterbalance

I was just back from the war, and my head was filled with marijuana and detached body parts. The former was somehow supposed to override the latter, but my brain wasn't having it. I was in Washington Square Park, and it was those wild hippy days, and my eyes fell upon a young woman with two daisies in her hair dancing with a young man in a wheelchair. There was a small radio on the ground and the music was soft and soulful. He knew how to lean the wheelchair back, just so, and turn it slightly this way and that as she moved with it/him in concert, her supple movements/his erasing the machinery below. There was a fluid grace beyond the metal or perhaps integrated into it, transforming its rigidity/my own as I watched and took another hit, deep and long and let it jet up into my head and thought: *this shit is finally working.*

Kamasutra for Virgins

They met on *Christian Mingle.com: Find God's Match for You* and were both saving it for marriage. It was their third date and they sat at the edge of a bluff after a long hike, and gazed at their small town below. He'd self-published a slim pamphlet he called *The Kamasutra for Virgins,* which was divided into three sections: FIRST BASE, SECOND BASE and THIRD BASE (with crudely drawn illustrations throughout), exploring a plethora of what he called, "God-sanctioned pre-marital pleasures" and handed it to her. When she got to the "Third Base" section she lingered, then stood. Told him she despised sports metaphors and flung the booklet over the ledge as they watched its meager wingspan flutter fecklessly in the wind, then he stood too. It was a long way down back to the car.

Squeezebox Serenade

He was from Brooklyn (never left it) but played a mean accordion in a Cajun band. She liked the way he said the word, *un-yion* instead of *onion*. But what she found endlessly irritating was the way he played Bach preludes for her on that giant squeezebox, like a serenade, in a tempo she found frantic. *It's important to know when limitations step up and bonk you on the head,* she'd think, *and vital.* Otherwise, she rather liked the sex just fine, and the way he related to her parrot. Never taking it personally when it shit on his shoulder or screeched: "No Bach!—No Bach!" or ever seemed to wonder where in the hell it might have picked that up.

Swimming Hole

As I passed through the village I saw the kids splashing playfully in the crater left from a 2,000-pound bomb. It was the monsoon season and the hole was filled with muddy water. Even at twenty I could feel in my gut the beauty of resilience and the horror of circumstance. My rifle was a crude wet part of me by then, an external organ. There was a lull in the incessant rain, but my boots bubbled with each footfall as we looked out for sinister things to step on, or secret hide-holes in the earth. At night the mosquitos were plump with malaria and our blood.

Coming Clean

Sometimes happiness is a moving target, Peter told himself without the words for it, as he sat across from his ex to work out some final details so late in life. He had told everyone who would listen that his father was killed in WWII. He said it with a crumpled face and with such conviction that he nearly believed it himself. In truth, his father abandoned them and married a young Italian gal, after rolling in on a tank, and had three kids with her who became pickpockets in Rome, and now he finally told his ex the truth. "Since we're coming clean," she told him, "remember that baby grand we had all those years ago?—well, I hopped in the sack with that piano tuner, but *just once,* and only once and never with anyone else, ever," and held up a finger for prideful emphasis. Peter stared at the bright red nail polish, relieved—happy to know he wasn't the reason the damn thing sounded like shit.

Meg Pokrass

Section Six

Luck

Her mother once said that a woman's luck isn't made in bed. "Don't believe a man when he tells you that myth," she said. But she lied. When a woman is handsome enough, she can smile bad luck right out of her body and into the body of a man with a hat. A man with a schoolboy's posture in bed will stare at a woman's trustworthy eyes and smile right back at his luck. She'll pop out those cheekbones, frog her wan face at him and watch him disappear into her sheets like tumbleweed.

Pictures of Extreme Discomfort

Calamity Jane slouching next to a nose-picking john with long legs.

Calamity Jane standing next to the kind of woman who feels comfortable wearing dresses.

Calamity Jane trying not to think about her suicidal sisters back home.

Calamity Jane missing her accident-prone mother.

Calamity Jane festering herself out of a sick early marriage.

Calamity Jane remembering to smile but only when drunk.

Girls

Wind in our faces, the two of us drove to the warmest part of the coast. It was beautiful there, hills smooth and set wide. The wind felt so warm, so right for it. "Put a bra on those mountains!" you hooted. Here we were, running away like kids together. Laughing about mountains that looked like breasts, even though both of mine were gone.

Let's Not Use the Word "Delicious"

The sound-soother is off. I don't any longer require tenderness and my big audition was years ago. I won't use the word "delicious" when I remember my husband's soft lips. The way it felt when he said my blue jeans *smelled like a forest.* How it started with vanilla bean coffee; pleasant and dumb. How, for the rest of our days, we swam in a sea of yard sales, flea markets, superstores, hunting for whatever would fit inside our dented red car.

Clouds before and after you were born

The day you were born, clouds flirted with each other. They had nice hair, ideas that led to better formations, blended into pleasant shapes.

But the day after you were born, clouds argued about some misunderstanding. In the middle of the night, they collided in the cold kitchen. The one, slouched over martini breath said, *Why do I frighten you?* The other in unwrinkled pajamas said, *Excuse me,* slipping past.

Bones

In the photo, my wife stood there kissing me, her breath a tangle of goodness. She had long been my hero, way before she was my wife, and you can see in the photo that she knew it. There was a bird fluttering between us, and when we stood right next to each other, the bird could finally rest. My wife had good bones, the bones of our child not yet in the picture—a child so strong he can fall from his bike in front of a car and not get crushed. When the photo was taken, we had just returned from a penny arcade. I had won my soon-to-be wife a teddy bear, and she kissed me as if she were kissing the bear itself.

Gone

It was fine this way, you told the dog, the day was new and fine and the sun was up now. Dad would not come home but Mom was fine with a band of light in her hair. Your mom, the dog, the sun. In spring, she used to say, an old dog will turn young. "For the best," she said. You sat up in bed and felt it—the lack. Your door, her door, the front door. His dog, who looked so sad.

As We Fade

We talk about how dandy our curtains look. How embarrassing they'd have seemed to us fifty years earlier. "Taste is the first thing to go," he says, sipping water like a bird. His eyeglass frames shine in the living room light. I wish to remember how our home feels when memory is gone. He coughs in the living room while I sing to the cats. We bake pumpkin seeds so that we can smell them baking.

The Wig Talks

After dark we went outside to see if we could spot any shooting stars. I made her head feel warmer. She told me this in her sweet and silky words.

"You warm me up," she said, patting me.

Tonight, we hoped for a real show, not last night's drippy lights from small planes. These days I find myself worrying about the woman below me, as though I were made of something else.

Extraterrestrial

There are no signs of extraterrestrial life, only two itchy dogs in the garden. One dog carries a blanket, lies down on it. Ma is sure she saw a spaceship float down into the neglected orchard after martinis last night. I'm on security patrol and my branch of the oak will be comfortable to sit on with a pomegranate and an orange. Carrying them in my pockets up to the lookout, scouting for aliens in the leaves. We'll move as the rent increases, but for now, sourwood sorrel invades our grass, fleas terrorize the dogs, and I imagine this house belonging to creatures who know what to do about life here on Earth.

Robert Scotellaro

Section Seven

Count On It

I'm in a Fat Elvis band, the older Elvis, pot-bellied in those glittery jump suits. My girlfriend, Riva, just broke up with me for a guy in a Skinny Johnny Cash band. She told me right before she left: "You want something you can count on, get an abacus!" I guess it's put a lot more twang in my guitar, that breakup, 'cause a cutie-pie from a Lit-Up Lady Gaga band and me have been seeing each other plenty. She says she loves the way I curl my lip at that crazy-sexy angle and the jump suits don't hurt either. Sometimes, when its real quiet late at night, when she's asleep, I use the abacus just to hear the beads tap together.

The Dentist and the Peanut Lady

She'd bring him peanuts every time she went over, worked for a company that supplied packets of them for airlines. He was a dentist in town who'd worked on her teeth and now they were what she liked telling her friends, "an item." They bickered a lot over petty things, and he'd remind her of the great smile he'd given her and how she should show it more often. They lived in a landlocked Midwestern town, and she found it ironic that he had a large collection of finely etched whale's teeth on his mantel and sang sea shanties in the shower. She hated peanuts but he made a big show of tossing them in the air and catching them in his mouth. When he got her the little 14k gold heart and anchor on a chain for her birthday, she wished just once he'd choke on the goddamn things he flung up like that; not die, of course, just have one good old fashioned, well-deserved scary choke for a bit, that's all.

Accompaniment

She follows me around playing a tuba, says it suits my disposition. I play a viola outside the shower stall as the sudsy water circles the drain at her feet. During canasta we play air guitar, for there's no accounting for the wiles of chance. The sitar she plays as I'm getting ready for work annoys me—hyperbole has always been an irritant. The musical saw I play as she's shaving her legs puts her nerves on edge, but in the sack, the cymbals are cherished, handed back and forth. And in the morning sometimes we play the timpani, after that second cup of coffee, just to keep us on our toes.

Interpreter of Dreams

My mother was the self-appointed interpreter of dreams, coughing out her verdicts with an early-morning smoke. Mining her slumber for forecasts: silverware meant guests were coming; hands, a gift; bees represented bad luck (especially if they were swarming), and "teeth"—the one we dreaded most—meant *certain death*. And it didn't matter whose: a family member, a neighbor, even old movie stars counted, were not safe, and we'd wait for the ax to fall, and of course it always did, and she'd say *See!* The Rosetta Stone she carried in her head, infallible back then. As we listened with our spoons frozen over cold bowls of cereal. She, in her robe, with her coffee and her cigarettes, and the fate of the world in her hands.

High Up/Low Down

He drove a monster truck in a big stadium on the weekends with the roar of engines and the crowds still in his ears days later. So high up, with such power under him, it was almost subterranean to sit in that overstuffed chair his father died in with a mystery book on his lap. A Mickey Spillane crime novel, he recalled, with a single match for a bookmark. Something about a shotgun hole in someone so big, a baby could crawl through without ever getting its shoulders wet. And nothing good on TV, and their old cat just peed in his slipper, and his wife was pecking at him from the kitchen about God-knew-what. And—*Christ!*—the weekend just couldn't come quickly enough.

A Penchant for Renegades

With a penchant for renegades, Beth dated a wrestler who wore a scary mask. Knew a lot about birds and said, when she was more interested in sex than facts, "There's a bird that uses farts to make worms come out of the ground." Said, "A mockingbird can copy many sounds; even dogs, machines too." Said, "There's a seagull that hunts whales, swoops down and takes bites out of them." Said, "There's a bird that drops a bug in the water, then eats the fish that eats the bug." He stopped to sip his beer—"Put the mask back on," Beth said.

Newfound

I bring home the wrong suitcase from the airport. It has a monocle, a black cape, and a book of prestidigitation tinged with dark arts in it. It takes a bit to learn how to keep the monocle in, and a good deal of squinting is required, but the cape is fetching and goes well with the pair of black chinos I break out. I somehow feel instantly transformed/powerful and a bit—strangely—aristocratic, as the cat glares at me suspiciously. Though a bit blurry, I read the book of magic through the monocle all day instead of going to work. I learn sleight of hand and how to levitate, while gravity slinks somewhere out of reach, and when my wife complains, with a wave of my cape, I make her disappear—well, not really, but yes, really too.

A Visit from Bad News

Bad News pulls up in his vintage shark-fin convertible with you in the passenger seat with your skirt hitched up to where I can see your new tattoo over the old one; a kind of pentimento. You introduce Bad News, say: "This is my new boyfriend, Good News." His cigarette flaps up and down as he says, "Pleased to meet you." His arm is around a new you and there is music in the way your clothes crinkle, and I realize Bad News can be a good thing turned inside out. Good News in his Bad News disguise guns it and peels off, as your hair waves a horizontal goodbye. There's a new pair of walking shoes I've been meaning to break in, tight so they'll pinch for a bit, but will shine up really fine, and that's the good news.

Excerpts from a Gangbanger's Diary

"Kicked this guy's ass today after school and think I broke his nose cause it sure looked like it was on crooked. Smoked a blunt with Dead Man and put the roach out in my palm just to show him I could. Sported my colors proud for Cecilia red like blood and she left the shape of those purple lips all over me. Heard there was a drive-by two blocks from my place stupid fucker was in the wrong place at the wrong time. I wrote a poem all gushy and shit for C and told her not to show it to ANYONE and made her swear on her mother's eyes. Took a peacock feather from my kid sister's room and put it in a beer bottle on my dresser and think it is real pretty but made sure I hid it when my friends came over."

Subterranean

He'd lost his job at the plant and was in the basement where his good-for-nothing teenage son lived. The father found the tightly rolled marijuana joints in a drawer and lit one. It had been many years since he'd smoked and he sat in the beanbag chair, a bit dazed, stared up at the window, which was ground-level and peered at a fat robin flapping about in a puddle of day-old rain. He had finally made it here, he thought: *subterranean,* and put on his son's virtual reality headset, the one that said, *Aladdin and the Forty Thieves (Cave of Riches)* and walked slowly through a cave, ceiling-high with gold coins, diamonds, ruby-encrusted goblets, and it was all his: there for the taking. He removed the headset, sat back down, saw that the robin had flown off, which, inexplicably, made him a little sad. He took the small bit that was left of the joint and smoked it, was going back in.

Meg Pokrass

Section Eight

Coral Reef Hotel

Dad in the suite, eyelids droopy, unforgiving; TV on, wine not as chilled as he likes. He wants to play Scrabble—like we do every night, but I want the man in the lobby, with electric eyes like an eel. When Dad falls asleep, I sidle down, plant myself near the Mermaid Bar. If Eel Eyes is hiding next to the bellboys with shifty legs or stuck in a crevice behind businessmen with loosened ties, I'll find him. I'll wait all night in the lobby, with the music of elevator bells. I'll dream about taking everything from my father.

Blood Lines

His words were phony, and I ate them anyway. Lemon curd, light yellow, incredibly fake. *Extraordinary,* I said to myself, moving like a god-damned lemming against his legs. His blood lines were, if anything, ruined. Best case: rare, brilliant, misunderstood wine or small-batch absinthe. What Alice sipped in order to grow small, sipping rabbit shadows all the way down.

Diet Commercial

Afternoon commercial for a diet plan: a woman's tongue licking a stalk of celery. She dances, sings that she's feeling free, holds a finger to her lips—"Shhhhh!"

This corner house feels dark. My clothes are cut loose. The tool which was once my body closes its eyes. The model's puny voice travels past my hips, hovers like a hungry neon bird.

Auld Lang Syne Syndrome

The doctor observes her for many weeks. Concludes that she is suffering from *auld lang syne syndrome*—a condition in which flecks of happiness are still present long after the reason for the happiness is gone. The sessions leave him missing his mother. Longing for the smell of her bread.

He writes notes that nobody but himself will ever read.

"The patient says that she can feel old buds of joy poking out from underneath her skin."

The Nice Christmas

The aunt guzzled three bottles of NyQuil. The mother couldn't stop crying and the kid hid in his hoodie all day. A marriage unwrapped itself under the tree, then croaked right next to the electric fireplace (Home Depot parking lot special).

Not one of them taught the dog to roll over and die. He just did—finally happy. On the very night Jesus was born.

Embracing the Waves

It was the first time she believed that the sea might not swallow her whole. It was the first time their bed felt softened by cotton, cotton inside the springs that had become softer and dumber each year—cotton stuffed up against his heart. It was the first night he told her he had been fighting the blues, and this is why he hit her harder, so that she felt the shredding of an old dream: a dream that a family like hers could make itself better—the dream worn to lint in the end.

It was the first time she felt that there were ways to sneak off into a glowing green morning, when the water wants you badly, and wants you still strong. She had always been good at seeing shades in a man, how they blended into each other. She patted herself on the soul, said, "you did good, you did what you could do here"—told herself that setting off in the silver-green waves was different than already being dead.

Twigs

For the past few years their sheets remained straight when he tried to court her. "When did you get that perfume?" he'd ask, but she wasn't wearing any or maybe she was and he didn't know it. Mornings, she was quiet, swaying in the wind of their living room. "Hey, did you fly away?" he said. That day, a nurse came in a car. Mostly, she remembered how his eyes were the color of marbles. She held that idea in her mind like a twig as he hunted around for her suitcase and slippers.

Empty Driveway

We ate potato salad and drank Italian sodas. All around us, sad-looking people walked happy-looking dogs. A dachshund never looks ruined. I let him slide his hand over my knee. Didn't blink, just sat there like an empty driveway. I had one hundred dollars left in my bank account, and my car needed everything.

Sex and Wild Seed

You handed me a bouquet of fake flowers you won at a ring toss booth. "Keep it," you said. It was the first time I understood how much liquid it takes for a flower to grow. And how a garden, with all of its inherent needs, would never be something you could take care of. I loved you back then because you smelled of sex and wild seed. I could see daisies knocking around in your eyes.

Extraction Dream

Tomorrow a dentist will remove a tooth, and under my tooth will be night noises; angry crickets, flu-ish frogs, grasshoppers. I'll ask about the roaring noises in my ears since the divorce. He will say something about allergies. I will smile as the dentist smiles. He will tenderly remove the roots so I can start over. He will call me "home" by accident, and in this way, my life will burst forth.

ROBERT SCOTELLARO

SECTION NINE

My Father Takes Up Juggling

He starts with raw eggs. Two at first, then three, eventually a dozen. We skate our way through the kitchen slime. When he snatches my misgivings and original thoughts, he flings them up into the air and there isn't a single one he catches. Outside he stands in the snowfall and tries to juggle every flake with a melting disappointment. Finally, he juggles the keys to his Cadillacs, expertly, in extravagant vertical orbits, pointing out the romance they have with light, that glint that blinds him even in the dark.

Paper Roses for the Fire God

She kept bringing him paper roses for that vase he had on the piano. But they kept turning into small torches, adding a twitchy stretch of shadows to the walls. After he'd been playing Rachmaninoff for great lengths, blackening the keys, she'd put on oven gloves and rubbed his shoulders. After a time, she let their canary out the window and replaced it with a windup tin toy parrot that enigmatically said, "tweet-tweet" when you wound it. When they watched TV she wrapped herself in tinfoil, trying not to make too much noise when she crossed and uncrossed her legs. Sometimes when she was particularly perturbed by his incendiary nature, she'd baste her epitaphs with kerosene and fling them at him just to watch them flare.

Adjustments

My ex sends me a risqué e-card again for my birthday, and it's actually good for a laugh. We "Like" each other on Facebook (our quirky posts) but it's a bit like liking the wind or a cloud that looks like a turtle or a frog; nothing personal. We've both moved on; she's got the bouncer behemoth she always wanted, and I've got the sensitive poet I've always wanted who knows her way around the alphabet. For extra cash my new girlfriend works at a music box factory and says the ditzy tunes get stuck in her head: a tinny tyranny that shoos away her best lines. Occasionally she sits on the washing machine with its monosyllabic regularity, to drown out those intrusive ditties when she writes. Sometimes when she smiles up at me with her pen poised, I wonder what refinements or adjustments my ex's bouncer dude, back from the blare and bluster, might find himself forced to make, if any.

Post Facto

She found the flip-books in a shoebox under his bed she never knew existed, like so much. It was all there: the bullying, the gender confusion, the monsters ... He'd drawn meticulously on each pad page, had calculated the slight positional differences that would give them movement, life—that simulated sense of it. As she flipped each page with her thumb, the stick figure history motion-pictured a small wind against her face. When the last one, half completed, was set in motion, it turned suddenly into blank pages. And it was then she noticed that searing bit of sunlight that had barged in through the window onto the lot of them.

Crosscurrents

That mourning dove was at it again, sad-sounding and insistent with its gloomy refrain. "I think it needs antidepressants," Susan said, "it doesn't even sound like a bird; you'd need twenty songbirds to offset that melancholy." I was listening to her with half an ear, what can happen when couples are together for decades piled high. I was thinking about the flies that circled our compost, how with a wave of the hand they disassembled, then reestablished their disrupted orbits with a renewed perky pestering; there was a metaphor there, perhaps, I didn't care to pursue. "I'm thinking of getting some Venus flytraps to put by the compost," I said, wishing I could patent the idea. "God, that same horrible complaint," she went on about that mordant bird, then: "Venus, Venus who?"—looked at me suspiciously—"I don't know any Venus; who the hell is Venus?"

Upper and Lower Universes

I'm a kid, and we're in my uncle's backyard, the two of us, and there are fireflies hauling their little lanterns around. His wife left him/my dad left me and my mom, so now we are stand-ins for each other's comfort. He points up at a falling star. "That's what happens," he says, "when the angels do pratfalls—they shake the stars loose." "What's a pratfall?" I ask, still focused on the lovely yellow stars in this lower universe, not looking up at all, and I can tell he can tell as he says, "Don't mind me." Years later I will learn what "pratfalls" are and real falls are. And be pained by the difference.

My Mother's Parting Words to My Father

Perhaps she said, as he packed his bags, "Those ornamental rooster wings of yours will never taste the sky." Or maybe it was "You're like a heaven where all the stars are made of mud." Then again, it could have been "I no longer seek your improbable wonders or those handfuls of powdered rust." Or possibly it was "I'm weary of listening to that peculiar squeak of an unoiled heart." Or it might have been "I'm no longer willing to dwell in your prevarications, which are like the one-room apartments spiders build." Oh, yeah, now I remember; it was "Get the fuck out!"

The Ghost Whisperer

She hires a Ghost Whisperer for her husband who, over the years, has become so faint she feels she could put a hand through him like mist all the way to the backrest of his recliner. The Ghost Whisperer shouts, "Hey!" but her husband does not respond. The TV news is reflected in miniature in the husband's bifocals, and he blinks. "Well, I guess he's not fully *transitioned* yet," the Ghost Whisperer says, "so I'll not charge you for the visit." The Ghost Whisperer notices, for the first time, that the wife must have had puffy lip injections as they curl into a glossy red smile, exposing way-too-perfect teeth. Just past her, outside a window, the Ghost Whisperer sees a bank of clouds formed into shapes, vaguely familiar, of a few old army buddies he used to know during the war.

Why Some Men Talk and Spit

There was a certain accent/linguistic variance to the men's spitting. Even the women, who didn't speak it, could tell. How heartache might be a throat-clearing bolt across the lawn. A bit of wistful reminiscence might be followed by a spritz through the teeth. The styles varied the way someone from a different province in the same country might say, "ketchup" or "caramel" with a slightly nuanced bend to the words. What concerned the men most was when one of them was down enough or drunk enough and the words were only followed by a sigh or a feckless *normal* swallow—that catapult of rage or sorrow turned in on itself.

Knotty Pine

On the eaves of the old cabin we were renting, icicles were melting in slow drips, as if water were waking from a deep sleep. Inside, you were in that fluffy blue robe feeding the fireplace like it was an endangered species. We'd quarreled about god knows what, and it was time for *us* to melt. The walls were knotty pine; all those knots, all those branches that could only be imagined. You turned and your robe swung open. "Hey," I said.

Meg Pokrass

Section Ten

The dog sniffed you out

The dog picked up the scent, and I followed her over to a cottage. The cottage was covered in ivy, and it looked as if nobody was home. *Nobody lives here,* I said to the dog, but the dog was crazy, acting like an animal, trying to find out the truth. I stood there in the sunshine and watched. The rain that had been spitting down on me seemed to have given up. And then the door to the cottage opened, and there you were, with those old taped-together glasses, your wonderful bloodshot eyes.

Moonlighting

Now you're answering his emails, filing his taxes, light-watering his purple-rose garden. When you finish walking his dog, he visits your new apartment, lands on the foot of your sofa like a silver-haired butterfly. "Great job with those ridiculous taxes," he says, a gentleman. Walks over and hugs you near your living-room window. What you don't say is that being squeezed by him is all you really wanted. When he lets go of you, you feel boneless—the tangle of your heart freed from its graveyard shift.

Cotton-Candy Truth

The cotton-candy machine buzzed like her teenaged boyfriends, sticky-coated con-boys, but she and the new husband lingered like flies. The clown in his Dayglo jacket staggered past, sallow-eyed, hungover, drooping. It came back to her then: the first time she'd walked into one of those tents. Then and now, the air was drunk on spun sugar. She smelled him first, then swiveled to look at the clown. "Dad, is that you?"

Moon Blindness

No sense in going all mopey-eyed, she tells herself, tired of moon-blindness and ready for more. She materializes in bed. Glimmers and stands out. The blinkers are on; her heart is warm. He is her phantom limb. And now she is showing him the moss all over her legs, showing him trees all over her shadows, showing him only the things her husband can't see—but he shuts his eyes, hums a little song, loses himself in wishes.

Paper-Doll Men

There was a warming shift when the new one appeared in her living room. Of slightly heavier construction than the last. Tired and slumped over, crooked glasses making his face look crooked. The eyes, behind glasses, waterlogged. Here is how she knew she was already in trouble—she couldn't stop feeling things around him. *I'm here to listen,* she said. The weight of such tear-soaked eyes might hold this one in place, she thought, still sad about the last one who blew away.

Fun Done

The ratio of sad men to happy men was tilting toward sad. Single men were claimed to not be attracted to anyone. They changed their names, dyed their hair, droned on about their dead cats. She was getting used to it. Howling in ecstasy, entwined during lovemaking, Bartholomew reminded her gently, "I am not available, honey; I just want to be clear." These new men were a parade of caramel-corn boxes someone had already taken the prizes from.

Wrong Birds

"Near the corner of the yard, I noticed those bright yellow birds again," he said. That was crap, she thought. The greyish birds around here were anything but. There was no way to know if he needed something else from her, and she checked the corners of his mouth. His smile had become slippery, so she focused her eyes on the branch of his nose. So sure of itself at one time, it pulled her right down from her tree.

Knee Deep

At night, the headlights of cars are like vacant eyes. I stand in the living room, knee-deep in life, and listen to the dogs in the neighborhood. I keep the photo of him in my kitchen drawer, on top of the potholders. He says, "I have always felt concerned about you." In the middle of the morning, he promises me popcorn with real butter, when I lose the weight. Some mornings he reminds me that I was an impossible person to touch, and I move him to a lower drawer—the one with the guest dishes.

Endorphins

Imagine how a rented BMW would elevate endorphins. Pulling up in front of the coffee store following his shift, saying "Hop in, tired man!" Rented BMW, rented dog in the back seat, rented mood flying on twelve espressos. Wearing a black sports bra, hefty new shades. Driving into the wind, parking in the Presidio to look out at the sea. Look at that rented dog, panting for whatever happened next.

Fillmore Street

She strides through the city with her Labradoodle, hair in a retro-sixties cut, cell phone plugged in her ears, ergonomic leather backpack. Smiles when people notice the sound of her special ringtone, chosen for her by the adolescent kids, (they've gone mad!).

Later, licking shotfuls of espresso with foam, sitting with a friend (talking about men like rivulets going nowhere or hair in soup) she says it softly: that cancer arrived like jellyfish on the beach overnight, invisible but real. Hard to believe.

"Here's the number for my Intuitive Healer," the friend says breathlessly. "Because hon, let's face it, there is nothing more boring than death."

Acknowledgments

Grateful acknowledgment is made to the following publications in which these stories or earlier versions previously appeared:

6S Anthology (edited by Lydia Davis): “Interpreter of Dreams”

10 By 10: “Coming Clean”

50-Word Stories: “Gifts,” “Whoopee, Hallelujah!” “Blood Lines”

100 Word Story: “Don't Bother, They're Here,” “Twigs”

As It Ought to Be: “at home when you aren't home anymore”

Big Other: “Luck,” “Pictures of Extreme Discomfort”

Blink Ink: “Knotty Pine”

Centaur: “Terror Tats”

Damn Sure Right: “Coral Reef Hotel” (Originally titled “The Lobby”)

Dogzplot, What We Know So Far: “High Up/Low Down” (under the title “Big”)

Duality: “Cotton-Candy Truth”

The Ekphrastic Review: “Embracing the Waves”

Elm Leaves Journal: “Counterbalance,” “Who We Are and Who We Wish to Be,” “The Cult Leader's Clockworks”

Fictive Dream: “The Proud Parents of Light,” “The Limits of Frost,” “A Treachery of Metaphors,” “Taboo,” “Spectacles,” “This Heat,” “5,000-Inch TV in the Rain”

Fortnightly Review: “Dwarves at the Door,” “Classic Movie Husband Arrival,” “Paper-Doll Men”

Funny Bone Anthology: “A Penchant for Renegades”

Ghost Parachute: “Acting School Lessons”

Gone Lawn: “Extraterrestrial,” “Heron Sighting”

Ink Sweat & Tears: “The Forest,” “Knee Deep”

Ovunque Siamo: “Atlas Wasn't Giving Anything Away,” “Dollhouse Furniture,” “Spectacles,” “Knotty Pine”

Paragraph Planet: "Gorillas"

People You Know by Heart: "Sex and Wild Seed"

Pure Slush Anthology–Loss: "Subterranean"

Pure Slush Anthology–Marriage: "Accompaniment," "Newfound," "The Jester"

Quick Adjustments: "Newfound, "The Whatchamacallit"

Right Hand Pointing: "Gone"

The San Franciscan: "The Whatchamacallit"

Six Sentences: "Dad Shadows," "Man Made of Hours," "Decanter Gig," "Gifts," "In the Flower Library," "Moonlighting"

South Florida Poetry Journal: "The Misfits," "Count On It," "Horney," "The Proud Parents of Light"

Switch Microfiction: "Bones"

Unbroken Journal: "Wings in the Living Room," "Cat Proposal," "Clouds before and after you were born"

Your Impossible Voice: "As We Fade"

About the Authors

Robert Scotellaro is the author of 8 flash fiction collections, including *Quick Adjustments* (Blue Light Press, 2023), *Ways to Read the World* (Scantic Books, 2022), and *God in a Can* (Bamboo Dart Press, 2022), and 5 collections of poetry. He has, along with James Thomas, co-edited *New Micro: Exceptionally Short Fiction,* published by W.W. Norton & Co. His work has appeared widely and is included in Norton's *Flash Fiction International* (2015) and *Flash Fiction America* (2023), and 7 *Best Small Fictions* and *Best Microfiction* award anthologies. He is the winner of *Zone 3*'s Rainmaker Prize in Poetry and the Blue Light Book Award for his fiction. Robert lives in San Francisco. www.robertscotellaro.com

Meg Pokrass is the author of 9 fiction collections, including *The Dog Looks Happy Upside Down* (Etruscan Press, 2015), *Spinning to Mars* (Blue Light Book Award, 2021) and *The First Law of Holes: New and Selected Stories* (Dzanc Books, 2024). Her work has appeared in magazines like *The New England Review, Electric Literature, McSweeney's, CRAFT, Five Points,* and has been anthologized in 4 *Best Small Fictions, Wigleaf Top 50,* and three Norton anthologies including *Flash Fiction International* (W.W. Norton, 2015), *New Micro: Exceptionally Short Fiction* (W.W. Norton, 2018), and *Flash Fiction America* (W.W. Norton, 2022). Meg is the Founding Editor of *Best Microfiction*. She lives in Inverness, Scotland.

www.ingramcontent.com/pod-product-compliance
Lightning Source LLC
LaVergne TN
LVHW051006080826
845145LV00009B/2483

* 9 7 8 1 9 5 2 3 3 5 8 4 6 *